MW00490196

**NEW SPORTS HEROES
FOR GIRLS**

A Drive to Win
The Story of Nancy Lieberman-Cline

*by Doreen and Michael Greenberg,
based on interviews with the athlete*

Illustrations by Phil Velikan

Wish Publishing
Terre Haute, Indiana
www.wishpublishing.com

LCCN: 00-102420

Book edited by Rick Frey
Proofread by Heather Lowhorn
Cover designed by Phil Velikan
Cover Photo provided by AP/WIDE WORLD PHOTOS

Printed in the United States of America
10 9 8 7 6 5 4 3 2 1

Published in the United States by
Wish Publishing
P.O. Box 10337
Terre Haute, IN 47801, USA
www.wishpublishing.com

Distributed in the United States by
Cardinal Publishers Group
Indianapolis, Indiana 46240

Acknowledgements

The life-long dedication of Carole Oglesby, Mariah Burton Nelson and Donna Lopiano to the promotion of women in sports has inspired us to write the *Anything You Can Do...* series. We'd like to thank the Women's Sports Foundation for its support and in particular the efforts of Yolanda Jackson.

Deepest thanks go to our editor Rick Frey who shared our vision to promote new heroes for young girls.

We are indebted to Michael Cohen, Jordan Shapiro, Arthur Seidel and Diann Cohen for their most helpful comments and criticisms.

Daniel Kron of SportsforWomen.com has been a wonderful resource and supportive friend.

We are forever grateful to our beautiful daughters, Alice and Jane, for their patience, example, advice and love.

We have always marveled, along with everyone else, at the awe-inspiring achievements of Jackie Joyner-Kersee and Julie Foudy. We are very proud that their insightful comments are part of our series.

Above all, we must thank Nancy, the hero of this book. Her talent, dedication and drive to win make her an example to readers young and old.

Finally, we wish to acknowledge the young girls who run and swim and shoot baskets and fence and play tennis and kick soccer balls and water ski and hit softballs. You look to the athletes who came before you for your inspiration. We look to you for the future.

Any errors of fact or omission are solely the responsibility of the authors. Michael believes that the mistakes are due to Doreen, and Doreen believes that they must be Michael's fault.

"I think little girls need to have big girls to look up to!"

— Teresa Edwards, five-time Olympian
& professional basketball player

Contents

Dear Reader,

The story of Nancy Lieberman-Cline is one of a series of exciting, true stories about female athletes. Nancy grew up wanting to play sports more than anything in the world. It was a time when most people, including Nancy's family, thought that sports were just for boys. Nancy would go on to become an Olympian, an All-American in college, a professional athlete and a Hall of Fame basketball player. Her life is an inspiration to young girls interested in the world of sports.

Doreen & Michael Greenberg

Dear Parent and Teacher,

Nancy Lieberman-Cline's story is one of excitement and inspiration. We invite you to read along and discuss with the young reader the triumphs and disappointments of Nancy's life. We know that participation in exercise and sports can bring many rewards to young girls including a higher sense of self-esteem and positive relationships with others. This is also an opportunity to engage in a discussion of those frustrations and anxieties that young athletes face at any level of competition.

We have attempted to raise some of the social and personal issues that girls and young women often confront every day. You are an important part of the process. Explore together. Read together. Talk together. Possible discussion questions, issues and resources can be found at the end of the book in the "Sports Talk" section. BEST OF ALL, Nancy's story is fascinating and a lot of fun to read.

Doreen & Michael Greenberg

Preface

by Julie Foudy

When I was in elementary school, all of my brothers' friends called me "Jimmy" because I was such a tomboy. I loved watching football and playing touch football. I loved watching the Los Angeles Lakers basketball team — those guys were my heroes... Magic, Worthy and Kareem. I would watch them dunk the ball and block shots. I wanted to emulate them, but a five-foot-tall girl had a hard time dunking the ball. I didn't have a Mia Hamm to watch on television. I didn't have a Jennifer Azzi to watch in the WNBA. And for sure, I did not have a Women's World Cup Soccer to watch on TV.

One of the lasting images of the Women's World Cup will be all the little girls watching women performing great feats in front of great crowds — painted faces and all. My special memory is an image of the huge smiles on all those painted faces. A dream became a reality. These same little girls are now thinking, "Hey, if Mia, Michele and Julie can do it, I can do it." Now, they are not only dreaming about a World Cup Trophy or an Olympic medal, they are believing in it.

For this reason precisely, all of us on the U.S. National Soccer Team realize the importance of being role models. We cherish the fact that we truly can make a difference in the lives of these children. We see it every day in their eyes and on their faces. We tell them to watch, to learn, and most importantly, to believe. If we can do it — they can do it. The reaction we get from them says it all... a huge smile and a high five.

JULIE FOUDY was a member and co-captain of the U.S. National Team that won the 1999 Federation Internationale de Football (FIFA) Women's World Cup. An 11-year veteran of the team, Foudy earned a gold medal in 1998 at the Goodwill Games. Foudy also was a captain of the U.S. National Team that won a gold medal at the 1996 Olympic Games and competed for the United States in the 1995 FIFA Women's World Cup, in which her team finished third. Foudy was a four-time NCAA All-American at Stanford University and was voted Most Valuable Player in 1989, 1990 and 1991. She was also a finalist for the Hermann Trophy in 1991 and 1992. Foudy is currently the president-elect of the Women's Sports Foundation.

Introduction

by Jackie Joyner-Kersee

More than 25 years ago, the Women's Sports Foundation was founded to promote the lifelong participation of girls and women in sports and fitness. We have been very successful, and we have seen many changes over the years. At that time only one in 27 girls played sports; now it's one in three. And that's because more and more opportunities exist to be a female athlete and also to follow female sports heroes.

Even with thousands of girls attending World Cup Soccer or cheering on their favorite WNBA team, we still have a long way to go. We need to get the message out to more girls. We need to let every girl know how great it feels to play sports and how very important it is to her whole being. We still have too many 11- and 12-year-old girls dropping out of sports or never even having had the chance to play at all. In fact, if a girl does not participate in sports by age 10, there is a less than 10 percent chance that she will be participating when she is 25.

Research suggests that girls who participate in sports have a real advantage over girls who do not.

Girls active in sports are more likely to be successful in school, less likely to get involved with drugs, and less likely to have an unwanted pregnancy. Sport and exercise can help to keep girls healthy, both physically and emotionally. The girl who is athletic feels stronger, eats and sleeps better, is more self-confident, and generally feels more positive about her life.

For a very long time, boys have had unlimited resources, such as books, movies, and games about sports and their favorite sports legends. Sport is where boys have traditionally learned about achieving, goal-setting, team-work and the pursuit of excellence. Girls and women should have these skills, too. We need to establish a large-scale network of resources about girls' sports and female athletes.

And we need to give girls their own heroes. "Anything You Can Do..." is unprecedented in its concept of offering real stories of new heroes to young girls. These are the adventures of young girls, coming from different backgrounds, who go on to achieve excellence in sports.

This series can open a whole new world for young girls. These books will give young girls a chance to explore the biographies of elite female athletes and their early sport experiences. The common thread that runs through all of these stories is a strong one — of perseverance and desire. Yet, each story is unique. Some are famous; some are not. Although the young reader may not always recognize the name of every athlete in the series, she may very well recognize herself, her friends and her teammates in these stories.

Doreen and Michael Greenberg bring to this series a long dedication to providing positive sport experiences for girls. I like their philosophy that it is not as important for the young reader to come away with the name of the person who won the big championship or the winning score, as an understanding of what it means to be a female athlete.

And by including the unique "Sports Talk" section in each book, Doreen has the opportunity to use her expertise as a sport psychology consultant and researcher to discuss important issues with parents and teachers. These are issues distinctive to girls in sports, including competing with the boys, making sacrifices, dealing with coaches, anxieties about winning and losing, and concerns about body image.

I am delighted that these books deal with a young girl's introduction to sports, the highs and lows of training and competition, and the reactions of family and friends, both positive and negative. It is so important for all of us to understand the young athlete as a complete person.

Most of all, the books in this series are fun and exciting to read. They will inspire girls to follow their dreams — whatever they are.

Jackie Joyner-Kersee was widely considered to be the best all-around female athlete in sports when she became the first woman to win back-to-back Olympic gold medals in the heptathlon at the 1988 and 1992 Olympic Games. The heptathlon is a grueling event in which athletes contest seven different events (100-meters, 100-meter hurdles, high jump, javelin, 200-meters, long jump and 800-meters) over the course of two days. A pulled hamstring forced her out of the heptathlon competition at the 1996 Olympic Games, but she came back to capture a bronze medal in the long jump. She also won a gold medal in the long jump at the 1988 Olympic Games, a silver medal in the heptathlon at the 1984 Olympic Games and a bronze in the long jump at the 1992 Olympic Games. She still holds the world record of 7,291 points in the heptathlon, which she set in 1988 at the Seoul Olympics.

1

Tip-Off

Just off Interstate Highway 91, as it runs through Springfield, Massachusetts, stands the William Naismith Memorial Basketball Hall of Fame. The afternoon sun reflects off the wall of glass which forms the front of the modern building. You can see the reflection of big white clouds in the glass floating between the giant cutouts of ball players jumping, passing and shooting on the front of the building.

A father and his young daughter enter the building. What a wonderful and exciting 10th birthday celebration it is for her. Last night she got to see a real life WNBA game at Madison Square Garden in New York City, in which the Detroit Shock beat the New York Liberty. And today her dad drove her all the way to this museum, built for people who love basketball, just like her.

They step off the elevator on the third floor and walk down the aisle, where red banners hang from the tall ceiling and bronze plaques on the walls honor the greatest players and coaches in the history of

basketball. Her dad points out Bill Russell, who led the Boston Celtics team to one championship season after another. There's Walt "Clyde" Frazier whose fantastic movements on the hardwood floor electrified New York City and the whole country. Another great member of the New York Knicks team, Willis Reed, is honored here, too. He showed everyone what it meant to be courageous on the court.

Then they see the name Julius Irving, the marvelous "Dr. J.," who seemed to walk on air. And of course, there's Magic Johnson, who really was a magician with the basketball. Michael Jordan's game jersey — Bulls # 23 — hangs in a glass case, and on the shelf to the right is displayed the ball with which Wilt "The Big Dipper" Chamberlain dunked his 30,000th point.

As the young girl roams among these many great faces, she wonders to herself, "Where are all the girl basketball players?" Just then, her dad takes her hand and says, "Now I want to show you something very special." They stop in front of the plaque with the face of a female basketball player. Her dad continues, "This girl learned to play basketball in Queens, just like you."

The ten-year-old reads the name out loud — "Nancy Lieberman-Cline."

"She became the youngest basketball player in Olympic History! And she is the one woman who, more than any other, changed the way the game of women's basketball is played," her dad says excitedly.

The young girl reads all about the great basketball player from Far Rockaway. She imagines this outstanding athlete shooting hoops in her own neighborhood.

The Rockaways are on a long piece of land that pokes out into the Atlantic Ocean at the edge of the section of New York City called Queens. It is an area that has always had neighborhoods of many different kinds of people living together. Far Rockaway is at one end.

It is in the schoolyards and playgrounds of Far Rockaway where Nancy Lieberman fell in love with basketball. Today, lots of girls love basketball, but, in the late 1960s, it was very unusual. Some people even thought that it was strange for a girl to love basketball the way Nancy did — with all her heart and soul, every waking moment and in every dream.

• • •

Mrs. Lieberman sat at her kitchen table in her home on Bayswater Avenue in Far Rockaway and prepared dinner. As she sliced vegetables, she looked out the kitchen window and watched the neighborhood boys playing football in the yard. All the kids came to play in the big open space that everyone called "Miniature Yankee Stadium." She laughed out loud at what she saw. It had rained last night and the kids were a mess — covered from head to toe with mud.

She could hear Cliff practicing the piano in the other room. She had to smile to herself as she thought about her son Cliff. "Cliffie's an angel," she thought. "He's getting all A's in school, and he plays the piano like a regular Van Cliburn." He was such a good boy. She really didn't need to worry so much about his asthma, because he took care of himself and spent most of the time studying and playing piano.

But her smile quickly turned to a frown. She looked out and saw that the late fall afternoon was becoming evening. It was getting cold. It was getting dark. She wondered to herself, "Where was Nancy?" Nancy was only 8 years old, and she should have been home by now.

"Nancy is Nancy," she thought. "All she wants to do is play ball. She must be going through a phase." She just didn't know what to do about Nancy. As she chopped the food for dinner and watched the boys playing outside, she grew more and more worried about her daughter. It was really getting dark. Where could she be?

One boy tucked the football under his arm and turned to run left. Then he stopped and ran around to the right. He seemed much faster than the other boys. He quickly ran down the field. "A home run!" thought Mrs. Lieberman, "or whatever they call it." She watched as the others jumped on top of him.

There was a big wiggly pile of squirming, muddy arms and legs. One by one they untangled themselves from the pile — Danny, then Hirsh and Scott and Jeff and then Eric.

Mrs. Lieberman glanced down the field. At the very bottom of the pile the last kid got up and held the football triumphantly in the air. His sweatshirt was full of mud. His face was full of mud. His red hair was full of mud.

"Oh, no!" Mrs. Lieberman shouted. She stuck her head out the kitchen window. "Nancy Lieberman, you get in here this very minute!"

"Aw, Mom, not yet — I just scored a touchdown."

"Right this very minute young lady!

● ● ●

Nancy sat on the front steps outside her house and waited for her Dad to pick her up in his car. Nancy didn't get to see much of her father now that her parents had split up and he had moved away. She was really looking forward to this special time they would spend together. She almost didn't mind that her mother had made her wear a frilly dress and shiny black shoes. Her mom had brushed her shoulder-length red hair and had tied it back with a green bow.

Nancy tried to wait patiently, but it was not easy. She got up and started bouncing a rubber "pinky ball" against the step. Nancy hoped her Dad would come soon before any of her pals saw her dressed up like this.

"Where was her father, anyway?" she thought. "He's supposed to be here by now." She threw the ball harder and harder against the front step. It bounced back faster and faster. She caught it first in her right hand and then in her left hand. "Where's Dad?" The ball went harder and harder and bounced faster and faster.

Her mother came out and stood on the top step. She looked down at her daughter. The ribbon in Nancy's hair had come undone. Her shiny black shoes were scuffed. She looked at the sad expression in Nancy's eyes.

"Oh, Nancy," said her mom. "It doesn't mean that he doesn't love you."

"I know that he loves me, Mom," said Nancy, still bouncing the ball against the step. "But, do you know something... sometimes that just isn't enough."

"Oh, Nancy," said Mrs. Lieberman. She stepped down to give her daughter a hug, but Nancy ran up the steps, brushing past her mom, and headed for the front door. As Nancy entered the front room, she jumped up to hit the door frame with her hand. She almost reached it.

● ● ●

Eight-year-old Nancy loved playing all kinds of sports — baseball, football, roller hockey, anything.

She just wanted to play — all the time. And when she wasn't playing, she was watching her favorite teams on the television. She was a big fan of the New York Jets football team. One day Nancy and her mother were shopping at a thrift store. Nancy spotted a used lamp that had a base in the shape of a New York Jets helmet. It looked just like a real helmet. Nancy begged her mother for the lamp. Her mom thought it was OK to get something to spruce up her daughter's room.

Only Nancy had no intention of using this special gift as a lamp. When she got home, she immediately disconnected the helmet from the rest of the lamp. Nancy ran outside to the kids playing football in a neighborhood game and put the helmet on her head. Now she really looked liked a football player, with her very own helmet.

It was not really a strong helmet, though. And it didn't have the protective padding. She was running back a kickoff and put her head down. As she hit the guy, Nancy's helmet exploded. After all, it was only made of thin plastic. She had the wind knocked out of her and fell down. Her whole head was hurting, but Nancy had too much pride to stop playing. She finished the game and went home with the broken pieces of the football helmet and an aching head.

● ● ●

"I got it! I got it!" shouted Nancy as she punched

the pocket of her fielder's mitt and squinted up into the late-afternoon sun. The ball plopped into her glove with a thud. Nancy pulled at the brim of her cap and trotted off the field, head down, like she had seen the Yankees' Bobby Mercer do on TV. In the spring, Nancy was playing sandlot baseball with the local boys everyday. Nancy was fast, and she had a strong arm. She liked to play left field where she could throw out any runner who tried to take an extra base.

She heard that there was a tryout for a Police Athletic League baseball team. Nancy was eager to make it on the team so she would get the chance to play baseball against kids from nearby towns. All the kids would get a PAL baseball cap and a PAL T-shirt. Best of all, they kept records of the kids' batting averages, just like the Yankees and Mets. Nancy liked the idea that she could see how good she really was compared to other players.

Nancy felt good about her chances of making the team. After all, she played with these guys all the time. She was selected for the team. She was going to be the starting left fielder and bat third in the batting order. Everything was set. But at practice one day, Coach Smitty said, "Nancy, I have to talk to you." Nancy, who was very excited about the baseball team, said, "When's the first game, Coach?"

And then the coach said, "Nancy, they're not gonna let you play."

"But, why?" Nancy questioned. She couldn't understand. "I'm one of the best players here."

"You are," said the coach. "But they can't let you play. The PAL team doesn't have insurance for girls."

"What are you talking about?" asked Nancy.

"I'm sorry, Nancy. Those are the rules. You are not going to be able to play on this boys' team."

"Come on, Smitty," Nancy said, "I'm going to be playing with these guys two hours later when practice is over, anyway! I'll be on the same field with them, playing the same game — just without a T-shirt that says PAL. What's the difference?"

The coach ended the conversation, "Nancy, there is nothing I can do."

The tough little girl who had been so happy about being picked for the team was very angry. She threw down her cap. She kicked her baseball glove.

"This isn't fair," she said to herself. "This just isn't fair at all." But a little girl does not know how to fight back against unfairness. Nancy picked up her glove and cap and slowly walked home.

●●●

Grandpa Lou and Grandma Eva were coming to dinner. Nancy came into the kitchen, dressed like always — in a T-shirt and cutoff shorts.

"Put on a dress!" her mother demanded. "You know Grandma likes to see you dressed up. You're such a pretty girl."

Nancy rolled her eyes. "Grandma likes to dress up with all that makeup and jewelry. I don't!"

During dinner, it was the same old thing — everybody making a big fuss over Cliff. It was all about Cliffie's good grades and Cliffie's piano playing. Finally, Nancy got up and started for the door.

Her mom asked, "Where are you going, miss?"

"I want to go out and play!"

"Enough with the ball-playing — stay inside tonight."

"Let her go, Renee," said Grandma Eva. "It's just a phase — she'll grow out of it."

Nancy started shouting, "It is not a phase! I like playing ball. You can't say that!"

"Stop screaming at your grandmother, young lady."

Suddenly, they were all drowned out by the sounds of loud piano playing. Grandpa Lou was sitting at the piano playing the "William Tell Overture." *Da Dum, Da Dum, Da Dum, Dum, Dum, Dum, Dum.* He played faster and faster, and louder and louder. Mom, Cliff, Nancy and Grandma Eva all looked at Grandpa Lou, and then they looked at each other. Grandpa Lou didn't say anything, but he had a funny smile on his face. Soon everyone was smiling. Then they were all laughing.

"Oh, Nancy," sighed Mrs. Lieberman.

2

Play Like a Girl

When Nancy was 9 years old, she watched some older boys playing basketball in the school gym. She liked all the different moves and the speed of the game. One night she was flipping channels and saw a basketball game for the first time on television. It was between the New York Knicks and the Milwaukee Bucks. She started watching. She was fascinated by the fast pace of the game. The players ran up and back, up and back — from one end of the court to the other. She was thrilled by the exciting way they tried to jump up and get the ball in the hoop and by how the other team kept trying to stop the players from shooting the ball.

Nancy thought out loud, "Wow, this game is great!" The next day as she was putting out the garbage, she noticed the headline in the newspaper — KNICKS BEAT BUCKS 109 TO 106. "This is so cool!" Nancy said reading about the high score.

During a recess period at Public School 104, Nancy went into the old and dingy gym. The boys were all playing basketball. She stood and watched for a little while. Then Nancy shouted, "I want to play!"

Everyone gave her a funny look, and the teacher said, "The girls are outside jumping rope and playing kickball, dear." But Nancy insisted on playing, and they finally said OK. She really didn't know how to play basketball, yet. She didn't even know the rules.

Mark threw Nancy the ball. As she started running down court toward the basket, her mind flooded with questions. "Now that I have the ball, what do I do next? Should I pass the ball? Should I try and shoot it in the basket? Do I stand here and dribble the ball and hope that someone will let me know what to do?" Nancy decided to pass the ball this time. Before too long, she was calling for the ball – eager to take the shot.

And from then on, every lunch hour and every recess, Nancy was either in the gym or in the schoolyard, learning how to play on the shorter basket. The schoolyard had two baskets – one 8 and a half feet high and one 10-feet high. And then she would run home and watch the Knicks or the Nets on television. She was starting to get a feel for the game. And she loved it.

She loved how quick the game was. The fast pace of the game was just perfect for Nancy. It was exciting when you had to make split-second decisions and really think on the run. In basketball there was the rapid changeover from offense to defense. At one end of the court Nancy and her teammates would try to shoot and score. Then they all ran down to the other end of the court to stop the other team from scoring. You had to be good at both.

So when the PAL baseball team wouldn't let her join, Nancy went straight to the Hartman "Y" in Far Rockaway. She went to the gym where the boys' basketball team was practicing. And they let her play. Nancy loved to play on the Hartman Y boys' basketball team. They had games on each Sunday. It was most of the same neighborhood kids — but now she had coaches, too.

She started to play street ball in pickup games in the neighborhood parks, schoolyards, and beach playgrounds. Some of these kids were different from her Bayswater neighborhood friends. They looked different and spoke and dressed in a different way. But these guys became her family. It was a family that was dependable, always wanted her, and picked her to be with them. They understood her.

• • •

By the time she was 10 years old she was getting really good. Everybody could see how talented she was at sports, and especially at basketball. Everyone noticed except her mom. Mrs. Lieberman did not get it.

Her mom would ask her, "How many home runs did you hit today, Nancy?"

And she would answer, "Mom, I played basketball today!"

"Well, how many touchdowns did you make?"

"Mom, that's football. I played basketball today! You know — with hoops and a big round ball." She just didn't get it.

There just wasn't enough time in the day for Nancy. For hours and hours every day Nancy would play basketball and practice her skills. Recess time always meant playing ball with the boys. PS 104 was only one and a half blocks from her house. After school she would bolt home, change her clothes, and be right back in the schoolyard.

Even at night she and the neighborhood boys would play what they called "Radar Ball" on the grounds of PS 104. As it grew dark, they would continue to play ball. All the light they had came from the one street light down the block. It would shine down and create deep shadows on the schoolyard. They could barely see the outlines of the pole, the backboard and the basket. And that was all they could see. So they would dribble the ball, shoot it and then listen. Did it hit the backboard? Did it sound like it hit the rim? And then they would run to where they thought the ball was in the dark.

Sometimes, they would miss the ball. It would roll away, and they couldn't find it. So someone would have to get up early the next morning and retrieve it.

17

Nancy was soon bringing all the guys home to her house for a quick lunch so they could have more time to play basketball. After all, she lived so close to the schoolyard and they lived miles away.

One day her mom started yelling, "Where do all these kids come from? You just can't keep bringing these strangers into my house! What will the neighbors say?"

Nancy said, "We're not doing anything wrong, Mom. We're just gonna eat lunch and go back outside and play. It doesn't matter to me if they're black or white, Mom. They're my friends."

• • •

Mrs. Lieberman reached for the ringing phone.

"Hello?"

"Hello, Mrs. Lieberman? This is the guidance counselor at Nancy's school."

"Yes — is everything all right? Is Nancy OK?"

"Well, yes and no, Mrs. Lieberman. I mean Nancy is not hurt or sick or anything like that. But, there was an incident in class during a math test."

"Oh?"

"Yes, well, to put it simply, Mrs. Lieberman, Nancy began quacking like a duck during the math test."

"A duck? Nancy was quacking like a duck... in class?"

"I'm afraid so, Mrs. Lieberman," said the counselor.

"That's not good," said Nancy's mom.

"No," replied the counselor. "It's not good at all."

"Why would she quack like a duck?" asked Mrs. Lieberman.

"Maybe she is just bored," the counselor answered, "or trying to get attention."

"Oh, Nancy," Mrs. Lieberman moaned. "What am I going to do about that girl? She's been going through this phase or something. All she wants to do is play ball — ball, ball, ball! I just don't know what to do."

That night, Nancy's mom called her into the kitchen and told her to sit down. "Nancy, you are going to have to stop this nonsense — playing in the dirt with all those strange boys."

Nancy insisted, "But, Mom, I'm gonna be the greatest basketball player one day!"

"Girls don't play sports!, Mrs. Lieberman answered firmly.

"Why?"

"Well, they don't."

"Why don't they?"

"Well, girls aren't supposed to do things like that. Boys play sports."

Nancy got up and put her hands on her hips. She turned and said, "Well, I am going to make history!" And she walked out of the kitchen.

• • •

Summer camp was not Nancy's idea. Mrs.

Lieberman had decided that it would be good for her children to get out of the hot city, so Nancy and Cliff were at Camp Surprise Lake.

"You'll get some fresh air, Nancy," her mom had said, "and make some new friends."

Nancy knew what her mom was really thinking. She was trying to keep Nancy away from the playground and all the guys she played ball with. She wanted Nancy to spend time with the girls at camp and be like them. "Bor-ring!" thought Nancy.

But Camp Surprise Lake wasn't so bad after all. It was kind of nice. They had lots of stuff to do — horseback riding, arts and crafts, and canoeing and swimming on the lake. The camp counselors did seem nice and a few of the girls were OK, too.

But there were two or three girls in Nancy's cabin who were always laughing and whispering among themselves, especially when Nancy walked by. These girls thought they knew all about the coolest stuff. One day, one of the girls called Nancy a tomboy. Then they all made fun of the way she dressed and teased her about how she liked sports.

Nancy told the girls to shut up and started pushing the girl who had called her a tomboy. The other girls started screaming. A counselor came and broke it up. Right away, she turned to Nancy and demanded an apology. Everyone was blaming Nancy for the fight. Nobody cared that they had started it by teasing her. Now, even some of the girls who had been nice to Nancy stopped being friendly.

Nancy waited for Cliff outside the mess hall where all the campers had lunch. Cliff was having a good time at camp. His asthma was much better. The boys got to play softball and basketball, which sounded like much more fun to Nancy. She told her brother about the fight. Cliff could see how sad Nancy was at camp.

"I have an idea, Nancy," said Cliff. "Here's the plan..."

That night, Nancy waited in her bed under the covers until midnight. Then, she slipped on her canvas boat shoes and pulled on a big, gray sweatshirt. From under her pillow, she took the big flashlight that Grandpa Lou had given her for camp. As quietly as she could, Nancy opened the front screen door, sneaked down the stone steps, and followed the gravel path down the hill to the lake. She checked her watch. It was almost 12:15. She looked across the lake, waiting for Cliff's signal. It was very, very dark. There were all sorts of strange, night noises — crickets and frogs and some kind of bird hooting.

Suddenly, on the other side of the lake, Nancy saw Cliff's signal — three quick flashes of light. She flashed back to Cliff. Nancy untied one of the rowboats that was fastened to the dock. She fitted the oars in the oarlocks and began rowing out to the middle of the lake to meet Cliff in his boat.

"Hey, this is really neat," said Nancy.

"Yeah," said Cliff, "it's a little spooky out here at night." They sat quietly for a while. They could hear the wind and the water lapping against the boats.

"I guess you really miss the playground and all the kids you play ball with, huh?"

"Cliff, I even miss Mom and Grandpa Lou and Grandma Eva," said Nancy.

Cliff laughed, "I never thought that I would hear you say that you missed Mom." They sat for a little while longer, enjoying their adventure. They were all alone in the middle of the lake, in the middle of the night.

Cliff broke the silence. "I guess we better get back to our bunks. This was neat, though."

"Real neat, Cliff."

Cliff began rowing back toward the boy's side of the camp. As Nancy began rowing back to the opposite shore of the lake, she thought she heard her brother say, "I love you." Buts maybe it was just the wind. Nancy couldn't be sure.

3

Queen of the Courts

Nancy had long ago hidden away all the dolls she had received as presents. They were in the back of the closet. Her room always looked like a tornado had hit — a really big tornado. There were dirty socks and t-shirts all over. There were dirty handprints up the walls. Nancy's hands were always dirty from playing ball outside, so practicing her jump shot in the house meant fingerprints and palm prints on the doors and walls.

When Nancy was 11 years old she could finally touch the 8-foot-high ceiling. It was a great feeling. Getting taller meant being more like Willis or Clyde or Dr. J.

Every night, Nancy was glued to the television set, watching the Knicks or the Yankees or the Mets. And when she wasn't watching sports on TV, she had the earplug of the little transistor radio in her ear — listening to the games. She would listen late into the night, until her mother would shout, "Go to sleep!" She took her sports teams very seriously. If the Knicks lost, Nancy thought it was because she had not been nice to her mother that day.

Nancy always knew exactly how the home teams were doing. Everyday when the newspaper came, she would cut out the standings of her favorite teams and tape them on a poster board that hung on her bedroom door.

Her room was starting to fill with posters of famous athletes. The light blue walls were being covered with her heroes — Walt Frazier of the New York Knicks; Joe Namath, quarterback of the New York Jets football team; and Muhammed Ali, heavyweight champion of the world.

Nancy just loved to see Muhammed Ali being interviewed on television. He would always tell you what he was going to do, who he was going to beat and how he would win. And then he would do it. He was not shy about claiming to be the greatest in the world. He was the greatest to Nancy.

Nancy felt that her room needed something else – a basketball hoop. But how was she going to get one? Certainly her mom wouldn't buy it! One day she noticed a whole pile of giveaway bumper stickers from the local radio station. There were maybe a hundred of them. She took them all. Nancy sat in her room and unpeeled them all and stuck them around two coat hangers. She had made two hoops. She used some cardboard for the backboard. Nancy nailed one above her closet. The other one went up on the other side of her room. Nancy had her very own basketball court.

When the weather was bad, the other kids from the neighborhood would come over and play full court basketball with a small rubber "pinky" ball in Nancy's room.

• • •

There were some things that Nancy wanted that her mother couldn't buy for her, or wouldn't buy for her because she thought that they "weren't for girls." All kids dream about getting stuff. But when Nancy was little, most girls weren't dreaming about Willis Reed basketballs or Chuck Taylor basketball shoes.

So Nancy decided to work for what she wanted the most. When she was 12 years old, she got a job delivering newspapers. Her delivery route for the *Long Island Press* had about one hundred houses on it. It was hard work. Then one day she had enough money for her first real basketball. She went right in the store and pointed to the Voit autographed Willis Reed ball, and said, "I want that one!" Nancy bounced it all the way home. It was a very special day.

When Nancy was 13 years old she worked at Playland Amusement Park for the summer. She worked at the concession stand cooking and selling french fries and burgers. Right next door was the basketball shooting game. People would pay a dollar and get the chance to try and make three baskets for a prize. Just being able to practice her shot was the prize for Nancy. She was spending so much time at the basketball stand that hungry people were lining up for food at her counter. Finally, the owner of Playland let her switch and she got to be in charge of the basketball game for the rest of the summer.

She saved enough money to get her first real pair of basketball shoes. She went right to Morton's Army-Navy Store and bought them. Nancy was very excited about her bright white, canvas Chuck Taylor Converse basketball shoes. She wore them everywhere. Some kids said to her, "What are you — a boy? Those are boys' shoes!" Nancy answered, "Yeah, but aren't they great?" It didn't matter that she got teased about them, because she was so very proud of her Chuck Taylors.

● ● ●

By the time Nancy got to junior high school she knew that she was a much better athlete than all the other girls and most of the boys. At PS 180 in Rockaway Beach, she was quickly becoming the best athlete in the class. In gym class she would get the highest scores on the physical fitness tests and she would win all the awards. Nancy wanted everyone to know how good she was. If you were supposed to hang on the bar for one minute, Nancy would hang for five minutes. She would always do more sit-ups and more push-ups than were required. She was always trying to win and win big.

Nancy was getting taller and stronger and more muscular. There had always been a lot of teasing from other kids about being a tomboy. She usually ignored it, although it did hurt her feelings. One day, in front of everyone, a girl tried to embarrass Nancy.

"Look at your arms!" the girl shrieked. "You're like a boy. Look at your muscles and veins sticking out!"

Before Nancy really knew what was happening, all the kids were shouting, and a teacher was pulling her off of the girl. She had decided not to let this girl, or any other kid, make fun of her athletic abilities. From that day on, Nancy was never embarrassed about how strong and athletic she looked, because it was part of being a great athlete. It was part of who Nancy was.

It was a tough time for the young, aspiring athlete. Most of the girls made fun of her, and no one in her family really took her sports seriously. It would have been great to have her parents or grandparents in the stands watching games, like other kids had.

Nancy used to ask her mom all the time about coming to see her play basketball. "Can you take me to practice?" she would ask. "I have a game tonight. Do you want to watch me play?" Nancy would ask her mom. But her mom always seemed to have an excuse. She had to make dinner or stay home with Cliff. It was hard for Nancy that her mom just didn't get it and didn't want to be there cheering for Nancy.

When Nancy was 13, someone special did come to watch her at a school tournament. He was very impressed with what he saw, and he came to talk to her after the game.

"Nancy, my name is LaVosier Lamar, and I coach an AAU team of basketball players in Manhattan. You should come and play with us. We do pretty well in the AAU competitions. Come see us. Play a little ball with us. We're up in Harlem. I can meet you at the train."

Nancy didn't hesitate because she had heard how good these girls were. "Great," she said. "Just tell me which subway to take." And the big, teddybear of a man started to laugh.

Nancy started taking the A-train after school, from Far Rockaway into Harlem. It was still New York, but it was a whole different world. This was the inner city — with all its noise and crowds of people. Her mother had begged her not to go to Harlem all by herself. She was afraid for her young daughter, all alone and a stranger to that part of New York City.

When she got to her stop, Lamar would be waiting to walk her to the park or the gym. She was always the only white girl there, but with a basketball in her hands, Nancy felt like she fit right in. Coach

Lamar taught Nancy a lot about playing competitive basketball. But, most important of all, he taught her to accept and respect all kinds of people — no matter where they came from.

The team Lamar coached was the New York Chuckles. The Chuckles were one of the best teams in the city. They called the new white girl with the red hair and the flashy basketball style "Fire." She quickly took her place as one of the best on the court. She would join any game that was playing. Everybody soon knew about the fantastic basketball player from Queens. Coach Lamar called Nancy the queen of Harlem; she was the player who could "get it all done."

• • •

Now, Nancy had to practice even more to learn the technical skills and to be good enough for the Chuckles' games. She would practice for hours in the gym and on the playground. She would dribble around orange traffic cones to get better at ball handling.

Nancy had seen a really smooth move on the playgrounds in Harlem. Coach Lamar had called it a crossover dribble. It was dribbling and switching the ball by bouncing it from one hand to the other. The cool part of it was the way it got the other team thinking you were going in one direction, and then, all of a sudden, you switch the ball to your other hand, and burst in the opposite direction.

There was a lot to remember. She had to do it without looking at the ball. Nancy had to keep her head up and, at the same time, keep the ball dribbling low to the ground. The footwork was tricky, too. One foot had to be ready to take off in the opposite direction. And she had to make sure that her free hand was always out protecting the ball from the other team. As Nancy practiced she would say to herself, "Stay low, protect the ball."

Even when there was bad weather, Nancy would practice. She would practice her jumps. She would practice her dribbling. It would drive her mother crazy to hear that ball bouncing in the house.

One rainy Saturday afternoon when Mrs. Lieberman was taking a nap, she was awakened by the loud, dull sounds of the basketball bouncing in the house.

"Nancy, please stop that noise in the house," her mom pleaded.

Bounce! Bounce! Bounce! Bounce! Nancy was practicing her crossover dribble in front of the mirror. She ignored her mom.

"Nancy, stop bouncing that ball!" her mom screamed. "I've got a splitting headache. Stop it already!"

"Sure, Mom. All right. In a minute, OK?" *Bounce! Bounce! Bounce!*

"Nancy, I'm warning you."

Nancy heard her mom's slippers shuffling down the hall. On her bedroom door she saw her mom's giant shadow, bundled in a heavy robe. In her hand Mom held a sharp, pointy object.

"I'm sorry Mom. OK. I'll stop. Really. Right now."

"I warned you, Nancy!"

Her mom raised the screwdriver. She plunged it down. She stabbed the ball again and again and again.

"Mom — no, no, don't do it," Nancy was shouting.

The basketball was dead. Squish. Flat. Nancy took off down the hall and ran down the stairs. She grabbed her baseball cap and rain slicker and escaped into the afternoon rain. Her angry tears ran down her cheeks mixing with raindrops.

● ● ●

Nancy was thundering down the court — left, right, spinning and dribbling the ball. She seemed to be doing pirouettes and flying through the air. It was the AAU championship tournament. There were girls from all over, from all five boroughs in the city. Nancy had felt nervous before this big game, but you couldn't tell when she was out on the court.

Coach Lamar had said, "Just play. Just do what you do. Just play ball." And he would point to the 4-foot high trophy for Most Valuable Player and say, "That's your trophy, Nancy. I don't know how we're

going to get it in the car — but that's going to be yours."

It was a very rough game. People were bumping each other and pushing, and elbows were flying everywhere. There were lots of people hooting and hollering. It was all so thrilling for Nancy. The New York Chuckles won. And Nancy was awarded the MVP trophy.

When Nancy and the coach walked in the house with the enormous trophy, Nancy's mom said, "Where did you get that?"

"Your daughter played so well, Mrs. L. She was the queen of the courts."

Nancy looked at the smile on her mother's face. She thought to herself, "I never felt especially pretty. I never felt as smart as Cliff. But playing basketball gives me a feeling like nothing else in the world." Now Mom and Cliff could be proud of Nancy, too. For the first time they saw that she really did have a special gift.

"I told you, Mom. Someday, I'm gonna be famous."

4

Out of the Cocoon

In high school the messy, scruffy Nancy became very, very neat. She was so proud of her high school basketball uniform that she would press it before each game. Her socks had to look nice, and she had to have her matching Puma basketball shoes looking good, too. She had wanted to wear #10, in honor of Walt Frazier, but #10 was used for the little kids. Willis Reed's number, 19, was already taken, so she picked #24 – Bill Bradley's number. Nancy was a devoted Knicks fan.

Her first high school coach was Larry Morse. He really taught her about teamwork. Basketball brought a sense of order and structure to Nancy's life. All around her kids were getting into trouble with drinking and smoking and drugs. Basketball kept her away from all that. Her coaches and their encouragement kept her focused on basketball.

Nancy was a terrific athlete at Far Rockaway High. She was the best player the Lady Seahorses ever had. She could run faster and jump much higher than anyone else. But some people were saying that she played too tough and aggressive. She played like the boys. She had street-ball toughness. She even loved to practice and played just as hard as in a competitive game. The other girls were not used to how hard she played.

Being the best was important to Nancy. She was always ready to show someone that she could be better. When they had drills at practice, Nancy was always the first in line. When the coach would tell them to practice shooting 100 layups, Nancy would always shoot 101 — first from the right side of the basket and then from the left side.

Nancy was always looking for a way to challenge herself. Each day she would dare herself to accomplish something. To be like Willis Reed, Nancy trained herself to play left-handed. All day she would pick things up with her left hand. She would force herself to write with her left hand. She would go into practice and say to herself, "Today, I am only going to throw left-handed passes." Soon, Nancy was able to pass and shoot the ball with either hand.

Nancy would set goals for herself every day and write them down. Whenever she thought of one, she would write it down — in her math notebook during class, on her hand while riding on the subway, anywhere. One new goal was to be able to pass the ball to her teammate without the other team knowing who it was going to. Nancy had to learn how to do a no-look pass. She decided to work on widening her peripheral, or outer, vision.

This was the drill that she practiced. She would stare at the scoreboard in the gym. Then she would hold her fingers out at the sides of her head and look for them, without turning her head. She wanted to see how far she could see without looking back — and all to help with her passing game.

• • •

Nancy continued to go to Harlem for basketball. She would get off the train at Adam Clayton Powell Boulevard and walk to Holcomb Rucker Park at 155th Street to watch the neighborhood guys playing pickup games. These guys were real good. One day, the spunky girl shouted, "Whose got next?"

They stopped and stared hard at Nancy.

"Say what?" one of the boys responded. He couldn't believe that this girl wanted to join their playground basketball game.

"Let the girl play," said a different boy. "Let's see what she can do."

She was soon a regular at the Rucker Playground. These guys in the playgrounds accepted Nancy because she could play, and she could play tough. It gave Nancy a lot of self-confidence to be able to hold her own with these guys. She got stronger and quicker. She learned some special moves.

Nancy complained to her friends on the courts in Harlem about how her high school teammates didn't like the rough way she played basketball. She told them that the girls protested about her street-ball style. The guys told her, "Don't come down to their level. Make them play up to your level."

She could play left-handed like Willis Reed, and she could be cocky like Clyde Frazier. Her tough, superior attitude would often get her into trouble. But it also kept her safe in the streets and neighborhoods of Harlem. The guys were always bigger and rougher in the playgrounds, so Nancy had to learn to take the elbows and give them back. And she wasn't shy about mouthing off to them, either. She could handle herself, and she earned everyone's respect.

Nancy would create mental games with herself to improve her game. She would imagine the crowds calling out her name. She could see the ball going into the net to score the winning point. She would use these mental games on the court, as well. She would never let someone on the other team know that she was tired or hurting. Her tough attitude and flashy style prevented her competitors from taking advantage of her.

● ● ●

When Nancy was 15, she saw a newspaper article about basketball tryouts at Queens College — for the USA Women's National Team. Anyone could come and try out. It sounded like a lot of fun to

USA Women's
National Team
Try-out Roster

1	5	11	16
2	20	12	30
3	32	13	46
4	17	14	42
5	51	15	63
6	14	16	
7	6	17	8
8	52	18	
9	38		
10	70		

Nancy, so a bunch of girls from Far Rockaway High School loaded up in a station wagon and drove to Queens College to play some ball.

What she saw when she stepped into the gym amazed and delighted Nancy. There were nearly 200 other girls and women there to try out for the team. Nancy had never seen so many female basketball players. She realized for the first time that she wasn't some kind of weirdo tomboy. She was an athlete and there were lots of other girls just like her.

Tryouts started at 10 a.m. Each player was given a number and put on a team. At noon, the coaches made the first cuts. They would post the numbers of the players who were successful up on the wall. Nancy's name was there. It just seemed like great fun to Nancy. She was just a kid playing the game she loved.

They made the cuts again at 2 p.m. and then again at four. Each time Nancy looked and still saw her number. At the end of the day, there were only 20 girls left. Then, the head coach announced the names of the final 10 who were going to Albuquerque, New Mexico, to train for the national team. The team was going to play against a team from Russia. She heard them call out "Nancy Lieberman." She couldn't believe it.

Nancy burst into the house. "Mom, Mom, I made the team! We're going to New Mexico, and then we're playing the Russians."

"What are you talking about? You're just a kid. You can't go to New Mexico. And besides, where are you going to get the money for the plane fare?"

There they were — Nancy's least favorite words, "You can't."

"Mom, you don't understand. I made the team. I'm only 15 years old, and I made the US National Team. I'm going to Albuquerque!"

Coach Larry Morse talked to her mom and grandparents. He said, "You'll regret it if you don't give her this chance." They said Nancy could go if Coach Morse went with her. Larry and Nancy's new high school coach, Brian Sackrowitz, and his wife Barbara helped to raise the money, to send Larry and Nancy to the USA Basketball camp in New Mexico.

It was so thrilling for Nancy. She was playing basketball with all the college All-Americans, the very best players in the whole country. It was exciting and hard work. Unfortunately, her stay at camp ended early because an elbow to her side fractured a rib. Although she was having a hard time breathing, Nancy continued playing with the pain for three days.

On the way to the airport, Alberta Cox, one of the coaches, said, "Now you go home and work on your game, because you're going to be a bright star one day. We're going to need you six years from now for the Olympics in 1980."

"1980?" Nancy challenged. "I'm gonna be on the 1976 Olympic team!"

When Nancy got home, Cliff was very excited and gave Nancy a big hug. It was the first time her brother had said to her, "You are one of the best players in the country."

● ● ●

Nancy dribbled an imaginary basketball into the kitchen. She fired a pass to an imaginary teammate to the right of the court (over by the stove), cutting down the lane (over by the refrigerator). Perfect pass. Easy layup. Two points. "Yes!" Nancy pumped her fist in the air in victory. Her mom was watching as she sat at the kitchen table, peeling potatoes and talking on the phone. She had seen Nancy win hundreds of imaginary games over the years — with perfect last-second passes and perfect last-second jump shots. She continued peeling away and talking on the phone.

Nancy was now searching around the kitchen. She looked behind cereal boxes in the cupboard. She looked behind the canned soups.

"Well, of course, Nancy plays center on her high school team, but she is so good that she can play any position in college," Mrs. Lieberman said to the caller.

Nancy was almost frantic now. Her head and shoulders were buried in the kitchen cabinet. She knocked over boxes of spaghetti and Jello and chocolate chip cookies.

"Outside shot? Sure, Nancy's got the best outside shot — and a great inside shot, too."

"Who is Mom talking to?" Nancy wondered.

"What is Nancy looking for?" wondered her mom.

"A-ha!" Nancy screamed. "Here it is on top of the refrigerator." Nancy pulled down a giant bag of red licorice twists. She ripped open the cellophane and stuffed two pieces into her mouth.

"Uh-oh," Nancy yelled. "Mom's talking to another college basketball coach."

Coaches from around the country had all heard about the redheaded girl from Far Rockaway, New York, who was playing basketball a whole new way. She played faster and tougher. It was the way she learned basketball, playing against the boys on the city playgrounds. She drove fiercely to the basket. She dove to the floor for loose balls. She pushed and shoved to get into position for rebounds.

Those who saw Nancy play knew that they were seeing the future of women's basketball. Letters were coming to the house from the coaches of many different colleges. They would phone all the time, too. They all wanted Nancy to play on their team. They knew that Nancy Lieberman could make their teams better and maybe even give them a chance to compete for the national championship.

Her mom pretended to be annoyed by all the calls and letters, but Nancy knew the truth. Her mom really loved it. She had appointed herself Nancy's unofficial sports agent. She took all the calls. She answered all the letters. Mrs. Lieberman was really enjoying all the attention that Nancy was getting.

"I like the zone defense over the man-to-man defense. But, of course, the man-to-man defense is nice, too. Nancy would be good at both."

"I don't believe it" Nancy sighed. "Who is this woman? I know she can't be my mother. My mother doesn't know the difference between a foul shot and a hockey puck!" Nancy rolled her eyes and crammed another red licorice twist into her mouth. "Next thing you know, she'll have me pitching at Yankee Stadium."

This was a very big decision for a teenager to make. Oh sure, her mom wanted to help, but Nancy knew that it was up to her. She was being given a wonderful opportunity — a chance to go to college and play basketball. She wanted to make the right choice.

Nancy knew that she wanted to go away to college. It was her chance to meet new people and live someplace different. It was time to begin a new chapter in her life as an athlete and as a young woman. She didn't want to go too far, though. She was still hoping to get back sometimes and visit with her mom and grandparents. And that was another thing. Grandpa Lou hadn't been feeling so well lately. She was worried about him.

● ● ●

Coach Pam Parsons from Old Dominion University came to Far Rockaway to speak with Nancy about attending school in Norfolk, Virginia, and becoming a Lady Monarch. Nancy, her mom, and the coach sat around the Lieberman kitchen table and talked long into the night. The university sounded great. Norfolk would be a wonderful place to live. And it was right on the ocean, just like Far Rockaway.

Coach Parsons told Nancy that she was putting together a great team and that with Nancy they could go all the way. Nancy was getting excited. She told the coach about the dream she had held since she was a little girl — of playing in Madison Square Garden like the New York Knicks. Coach Parsons said that they could schedule some games against New York schools and maybe play in the Garden. Nancy wanted a chance to play in front of Mom and her grandparents and her pals from the playgrounds.

Now Nancy was really interested in Old Dominion. Nancy hoped that this would be a good match and that she and Coach Parsons would get along.

Then, a coach from another school phoned Nancy. He told her, "If you go to a school like Old Dominion, you'll never be an All-American, never win a national championship."

"Oh, yeah?" Nancy thought to herself. "I'll show you. I'll show everyone. Maybe you haven't heard about Old Dominion yet, but soon it will be the best women's basketball team in the whole country."

He probably should have talked to Mrs. Lieberman before he spoke with Nancy. The surest way to get Nancy to do something was to tell her it couldn't be done. Just ask her mom.

5

A Silver Lining

Nancy was only 17 years old and a high school senior when she tried out for the U.S. Olympic women's basketball team in Warrensburg, Missouri. Most of the others trying out were already stars on their college teams, and several were All-Americans. Nancy knew she would have to play as hard as she possibly could. But, of course, she always did.

Billie Moore of Cal-State Fullerton was the head coach selecting the U.S. team. She wanted her players to be really tough when they took on the world's best at the Olympic Games. So she was making these tryouts extra hard. They had to run, run and run some more. Nancy had never run so much in her life. Passing drills. Shooting drills. Defense. More running. Nancy didn't know that she could be this tired and still continue to play. She was in the best shape of her life. She was stronger and faster than she had ever been.

During a short break in the morning practice, Nancy collapsed in a heap in a corner of the gym. Drops of sweat poured on the hardwood floor, forming puddles around her. As she gulped down some water, she wrote in her diary:

We went 2 hours this morning — I believe they're crazy — yes, the coaches — we ran 3-man weave, 5-man weave, 3-on-2, 2-on-1, 11-man drill, shooting, man defense, zone defense, deny, head on ball, full-court 1-on-1, then - "Ladies, let's scrimmage." Scrimmage? — I can't breathe or walk. Need some sleep. Next practice at 2:00.[1]

Day by day, the tension seemed to build. Only 12 of these female basketball players would make the Olympic team. Every single one of them was a terrific athletic and a skilled basketball player. Nancy had never been this nervous. They were all waiting to see who was picked. She couldn't wait any longer. She thought that she would explode. Nancy would have preferred to be trying to make the last second shot in a tie game.

There was a shout down the hall. Everyone ran. There were screams and tears. One of the assistant coaches had thumb-tacked the list of the final team members to the bulletin board.

Nancy held her breath as she quickly scanned the list for her name. "Please, please!" she prayed. "Yes!" There it was:

---

[1]Lieberman-Cline, Nancy with Debby Jennings. *Lady Magic: The Autobiography of Nancy Lieberman-Cline,* Sagamore Publishing, 1982 ; p. 58.

LIEBERMAN, NANCY

"A phone. I need a phone — I've got to call Mom, and Cliff and Grandpa Lou and Grandma Eva. I made the team! I'm going to the Olympics!"

Nancy Lieberman celebrated her 18th birthday at the Olympic trials in Hamilton, Ontario, Canada. At the little party her teammates threw for her, they had ice cream and a cake, and they put her hair up in braids. Nancy had never felt so happy or looked so silly.

• • •

It was the start of the 1976 Olympic Games in Montreal, Canada. The U.S. team members stood in the tunnel below the Olympic Stadium. They were ready to march in the opening ceremonies. Proudly, Nancy stood in her white hat and red, white and blue suit. Only it didn't make sense to her that they had to wear these silly dressy shoes. Her feet were squished. Why couldn't she wear her basketball shoes? Suddenly, they were moving — marching through the tunnel and out onto the field of Olympic Stadium.

The sky was lit by thousands of colorful rockets. *The Star-Spangled Banner* began to play. The roar from the spectators seats was deafening. Nancy was proud and happy. She walked side by side with thousands of other athletes there to represent their countries and try their best. Nancy looked up and saw the American flag swirling in the night breeze. For a few minutes, she almost forgot how much her feet hurt.

Nancy loved living in the Olympic village among her fellow athletes. She enjoyed the friendship of her teammates as they sat around the dining hall, laughing and joking into the night. Athletes from many different countries would trade hats and T-shirts and wristbands and pins with each other. They would take them back home as souvenirs of the wonderful experience they all shared together.

Nancy turned out to be a pretty good trader. The athletes from Russia and the other Eastern European countries loved American blue jeans. Nancy had brought along a few extra pairs from home to swap. Before long, Nancy could be seen walking around the village with her white USA sailor's cap, covered with a hundred souvenir pins showing the symbols and colors of teams from all over the world.

One day, Nancy got into a crowded elevator. Next to her was a little Romanian girl. She had a brown ponytail and big brown eyes, and she was hugging a teddy bear.

"Boy," Nancy thought. "What a big baby! A teddy bear at the Olympics. Better toughen up, little girl, if you want to play with the big kids."

Well, it turned out that the little Romanian with the big teddy bear was Nadia Comenici, and a few days later the whole world would know who she

was. She scored the first perfect 10 in the history of Olympic gymnastics. She became a hero to thousands of little girls in her own country and all over the world. Nancy was a little embarrassed when word of Nadia's great accomplishment spread around the Olympic village.

"I guess she was a lot tougher than she looked," Nancy thought to herself. Nancy would always remember this little lesson and never again judge people by first appearances.

"It's how tough you are when it really counts that matters."

● ● ●

Sometimes the problems and the troubles of the real world intruded into this wonderful place of hope and friendship. Four years earlier, at the 1972 Munich Olympics, terrorists with guns had broken into the village. They kidnapped members of the Israeli wrestling team, and 11 athletes were murdered as the world looked on in horror.

Here in Montreal, guards walked around the Olympic village all day and all night. Some carried long rifles with pointy bayonets fixed on the end. Some carried scary looking machine guns. The guards with the guns made Nancy nervous and uncomfortable. She had a funny feeling in the pit of her stomach.

● ● ●

The first game was at 9 a.m. Nancy was the youngest player on the American team and the only one who wasn't a collegiate star. She wasn't one of the starters, and she didn't really expect Coach Moore to play her very much. She sat on the end of the bench in her blue uniform with the red and white "USA" and the big number "10" after her idol on the Knicks, Walt Frazier. She was still as proud as she could be.

She cheered for her teammates — Ann Meyers, Pat Head, Lusia Harris, and Julienne Simpson. She clapped loudly whenever they scored or made a good play on defense. The team played hard but was beaten by opening-round jitters and a very well-trained Japanese team.

They rallied and won the next two contests beating a good-shooting Bulgarian team and the Canadians, who were the home team. The next game would be against the team from the Soviet Union. They were the biggest and most experienced team, and most people thought that the Soviets would easily win the Olympic gold medal.

Nancy's mom was in the stands, and so were Nancy's old friends Mark and Eric Muchnik, and her high school teammate Annie Nisenholc. They came all the way from Far Rockaway, New York to Montreal to cheer for Nancy and the whole USA team.

"Oh, gosh!" thought Nancy as she jogged out onto

the court to begin warm-ups. "I had heard these players were big, but..." As they formed two lines and began to shoot layups, it was hard for the Americans to keep from staring. The starting center on the Soviet team, Uljana Semjonova, was 7 feet 2 inches tall and weighed about 260 pounds.

"Focus, ladies," shouted Coach Moore. "Just play our game. Let's not worry about the other guys."

"Yeah, right," thought Nancy, as she took her seat at the end of the bench. "Easy for you to say. No chance Lieberman's going to get into this game," Nancy said to herself.

Not only were the Soviets big, but they were tough, throwing around their elbows when they went up for rebounds. They would stick out their behinds whenever anyone tried to drive the lane. And not only were they tough, but they were good, too.

After just a couple of minutes of play, the Soviet team had taken a 17-4 lead in the game. They looked unstoppable.

"Lieberman," shouted Coach Moore. "Get in there and take the back end of the one-three-one zone."

"What? Did she really say Lieberman?" Nancy wondered. "She really must be desperate."

Nancy stepped out of her warm-up sweats and bravely trotted out to take her position. The knot in her stomach clenched tighter and tighter.

Nancy caught a pass at the top of the lane and quickly fired it under the basket. It bounced off the knee of a surprised teammate and into the hands of a Soviet player. Nancy spun around and ran back on defense as fast as she could. It was a two-on-one break. Nancy took her position underneath the Soviet basket. She'd show them. She was tough. She would hold her ground no matter what.

Nancy reached out to try and steal the pass from the Soviet guard. She missed. The guard shovelled the ball to the giant center who was charging down the court at full speed. For a split second, Nancy was thinking, "Lieberman, what have you gotten yourself into now?" She looked up just in time to see the freight train named Semjonova chugging down the track. Then she heard a loud crunch. Everything started to spin. And then... nothing. Nancy was out cold.

"Don't move!" shouted the team trainer.

"Nancy, stay still," advised Coach Billie Moore.

Little by little, Nancy began to regain consciousness. It was like swimming back to the surface after a long dive down to the bottom of the lake. Mrs. Lieberman was frantically trying to make her way through the rows of seats and down onto the floor. Nancy was back on her feet, though still a little wobbly. Her coach and trainer helped her off the court

• • •

"Ladies, this is not just a basketball game. Tonight, you are playing for the history of women's basket-

ball. You will change the course of our sport, when you have that medal placed around your neck tonight."

Coach Moore looked around the locker room as her team finished suiting up for the all important medal game against Czechoslovakia. The winner of the game would earn a silver medal for themselves, their team and their country. They would be part of the very first medal winners for women's basketball in Olympic history.

Nancy looked up from lacing her sneakers. Usually, the red-haired kid from Queens could be counted on for a wisecrack remark. But on this night, she looked her coach in the eye and gave her a small, confident nod of the head. They were ready.

Over 17,000 people jammed into the Montreal Forum. The USA team played their best game of the Olympics. They got out to an early lead. Then they got into some trouble as the Czechs made a run at them in the second half of the game. The USA team hung in for the victory. The buzzer sounded and the crowd were on their feet, stamping and clapping.

"U S A, U S A, U S A," they shouted. Nancy ran out onto the court. She hugged her teammates. She hugged her coaches. She hugged strangers. Nancy looked around and tried to find her mom among the wildly cheering fans in the Forum. It was a wonderful, crazy dream come true.

Nancy and her teammates stood on the platform for the silver medal winners. They proudly held their right hands over their hearts as they heard *The Star-Spangled Banner* played and watched the American flag being raised. They waved jubilantly to the crowd. They would never forget what they had accomplished together.

After the medal ceremony, one member of each medal-winning team was chosen at random, to be tested for drug use. Guess who they picked? That's right. Nancy had to accompany a female security guard back to the locker room and pee in a bottle. The sample would be tested to make sure no one was using any illegal chemicals. No one got to take home her shiny silver medal until Nancy peed in front of the security guard. Well, she was so nervous and embarrassed that she couldn't do it. Nancy drank some water. She looked at the ceiling. She drank some more water. She whistled a tune. She drank some more water. Finally...

"Good thing the Olympic Committee isn't testing for red licorice," Nancy thought to herself. She ran out of the locker room, her silver medal dangling around her neck.

● ● ●

Back in Far Rockaway, all her friends and relatives stopped by to congratulate Nancy. Mom was so proud. There was a "Nancy Lieberman Day" in

Queens and a special night at Yankee Stadium. At the start of the Yankees' game, the scoreboard in left center field lit up with the message:

THE NEW YORK YANKEES

WELCOME

FAR ROCKAWAY OLYMPIAN

NANCY LIEBERMAN

Nancy stood up in her seat behind the home team dugout and threw out the first ball.

6

"We're Number One!"

It could have been the most wonderful year. It should have been great. Nancy was a freshman at a great university. She was living on her own. She was doing well. Nancy was the star forward on a basketball team of talented athletes, a team that was gaining fans all over. It should have been terrific — but it wasn't.

Things got off to a bad start. Nancy was physically run down from the hard pace of the Olympic training schedule. When she came to Old Dominion as a freshman in the fall, she tried hard to balance her studies with basketball practice. Maybe she was doing too much. She developed a case of mononucleosis — a low-grade infection with a fever, that left her tired and weak. Nancy was forced to miss the first several games of the season. And when she did come back, she came back too soon. Her body wasn't ready for the tough challenge.

The team lost their first game to North Carolina State. Coach Parsons called Nancy, who was home sick in bed, at midnight to tell her about the loss.

Nancy felt that Coach Parsons was blaming her for the way the team played. Didn't she know that Nancy would have done anything to be there playing with her teammates?

It seemed to Nancy that the coach was trying to come between her and the other players on the team. One day the coach would be praising Nancy and the next day she would be calling her names in front of everyone. Sometimes the coach wanted Nancy to be the star. "Play like Lieberman," Coach would tell the team. "After all, isn't she the one the sports' reporters all want to write about? Isn't she the girl with the Olympic silver medal around her neck?"

It put Nancy in a bad spot. Nancy knew that she was only a freshman. And she really didn't feel like a team leader so early in her college career. She just wanted to fit in with her teammates. If she didn't try to be the leader, she might be letting down the team. If she did try to be the leader, people would think she had a big head.

There was constant yelling and cursing from the coach. Nancy had to tune it all out and just play basketball. Coach Parsons had given Nancy a hard time about being sick. She always seemed to be really jealous about Nancy's Olympic accomplishment. Playing basketball under Coach Parsons was torture for Nancy.

Nancy and Coach Parsons just were not getting along. Not on the court. Not off the court. Pam Parsons was the reason that Nancy had chosen Old Dominion University. If Coach Parsons didn't trust Nancy, if she didn't like Nancy, well then, who did?

In the past, Nancy had always had basketball. If she was having a problem with her mom — there was basketball. If she was having a problem at school — there was basketball. On the basketball court Nancy had always felt comfortable. She knew she was good. She felt safe and accepted. But now, with this mess between Coach Parsons and herself, basketball was the problem. Nancy really didn't know how to handle this.

The sports pages would tell the story of a most successful season, both for the team and for Nancy. The Lady Monarchs won 23 games and lost only nine. They were the champions for the state of Virginia. Nancy had averaged 21 points a game. But for Nancy, the whole season had been one long nightmare.

Clang! Nancy slammed shut her locker door. She had cleaned out everything from her locker, piling her sneakers and sweats into a cardboard box. "I don't know if I'll be back next year," thought Nancy. "This just isn't fun any more."

Nancy's world was spinning out of control. She didn't think she could feel much lower. A few weeks later Nancy got a late-night phone call. Grandpa Lou had died.

• • •

"OK ladies, good work, good work," Coach Pat Head called out to the 12 girls scrimmaging on the court. "Tomorrow we'll take it up another notch." Several of the players groaned and made a sound something like "Ugggh." Most of them looked too tired to fall down.

"Let's take 20 foul shots, run around the court 10 times, and then hit the showers. Nancy, I'd like to see you for a minute."

Nancy and Pat took seats high up in the bleachers overlooking the girls practicing their foul shots. Pat had been the co-captain of last year's Olympic team. She then became the coach at the University of Tennessee. This summer she was coaching the U.S. Junior National Team.

Pat had heard about the problems Nancy was having with her old coach. She had invited Nancy to become part of the junior national team. Pat didn't want Nancy to give up on basketball. Nancy was training as hard as she ever had. She was playing well. But, most important, her love of basketball had returned — stronger than ever.

"I think that you and your new coach at Old Dominion, Marianne Stanley, will work well together. I believe that the future holds great things in store for you. Call it a hunch."

Nancy nodded her head and smiled. She started to make her way down the bleacher steps.

"Oh, Nancy — one more thing. If Old Dominion

plays Tennessee in the tournament, take it easy on us, will you?"

Nancy laughed.

"And another thing." Coach Head gave Nancy a very fierce and intense stare. "Don't forget to take your 20 foul shots."

"Yes, ma'am." Nancy gave a pretend salute, and ran down the steps onto the court.

● ● ●

The new women's basketball coach at Old Dominion was Marianne Crawford Stanley. Marianne had been the point guard on the Immaculata College championship team. She had tried out for the Olympic team going to Montreal, but she was the last player cut from the squad. The Olympic coaches had chosen a high school kid to be the 12th player on the team — a redhead from Far Rockaway, New York.

The players were starting to come together as a team. Nancy couldn't wait to come to practice each day. There was a whole new feeling on the court and in the locker room. Nancy was starting to have that old dream again - the dream of a national championship. It was a dream that Nancy was happy to share with her teammates, most of the students at Old Dominion, and many of the citizens of Norfolk, Virginia. Tickets at home games were getting hard to come by. Everyone wanted to come and see this exciting team play.

"Wow! Lieberman's got to be about the luckiest basketball player I've ever seen." A big guy wearing an Old Dominion sweat shirt and an Old Dominion baseball hat jumped up screaming, spilling his coke and dumping his popcorn on the fans seated around him. Nancy had just made an unbelievably fantastic shot from half-court with just two seconds left to win the game.

What that big guy didn't know, of course, was that Nancy had been practicing that shot since she was 10 years old. Nancy had found out long ago that the "luckiest" players turned out to be the ones who practiced the most and who played the hardest.

● ● ●

One day after practice, Coach Stanley called Nancy into her office. Nancy showered quickly and took a seat with her hair still wet and a towel around her neck.

"Nancy, I'm moving you out to point guard."

Nancy was surprised. "But why? I'm playing well. I'm scoring 20 points a game and the team is winning."

"Nancy, you've been great. But if we're going to achieve our goal, if we're going to go for the national championship, I need to get as much from everyone else on the team as I'm getting from you. As a point guard, you will be like a coach on the court. Maybe you'll score fewer points, but I guarantee you — the Lady Monarchs will win more games."

Nancy began to think about basketball in a whole new way. She understood that the coach needed her to help make everyone on the court better. The strategy worked. Old Dominion's big center, Inge Nissen, and Nancy soon became the best inside-outside combination in women's college basketball.

Time and again, Nancy would drive to the basket. If the opposing center would come out to double-team Nancy, she would bounce the ball to Inge for an easy shot. If the opposing center stayed back, Nancy could either drive to the hoop or dish it out to an open teammate on the side. With Nancy as the point guard, opposing teams had a much harder time trying to keep the Lady Monarchs from scoring. Nancy was loving it. Playing the point was a lot of fun. Winning was fun, too.

● ● ●

Nancy was soon playing point guard like no one else — well, almost like no one else. She was making left-handed passes, behind-the-back passes, through-her-legs passes. One day the Michigan State men's team came to Old Dominion to play in a tournament. The Michigan State Spartans were led by their own point guard, Ervin "Magic" Johnson, already one of the best college players in the country. He was already showing the great skills and magical moves that would one day make him an NBA all-star and hall-of-famer.

Magic made a fantastic behind-the-back pass that brought everyone in the arena to their feet with a look of amazement on their faces. One balding sportswriter with a rolled-up game program in his hand and a big grin on his face turned to the female sportswriter next to him.

"Our Nancy Lieberman plays just like Magic Johnson," he said to her.

"No," she answered with a big smile of her own, "Magic Johnson plays just like Nancy Lieberman." From that day forward, the reporters began nick-naming Nancy, "Lady Magic."

• • •

Nancy was playing great. The team was playing great. It was Nancy's junior year at Old Dominion. Everyone said she was sure to be named as a first team All-American. With the addition of sharp-shooting freshman Rhonda Rompola playing the other guard position, it was almost impossible to stop the Lady Monarchs. Everyone thought that they might have a chance to go all the way to the National Championship.

Nancy was excited. The team was travelling to New York to play Queens College late in the season. The game would be played in Madison Square Garden, the home of her childhood heroes — the New York Knicks. She would be playing in front of her family and friends. But Nancy was a little sad, as well. Tomorrow would have been Grandpa Lou's birthday. She knew that he would have wanted to be at the Garden to see her play and cheer her on. Nancy really missed Grandpa Lou.

Nancy was sitting in the locker room, tightening her shoelaces and preparing to run out through the tunnel and out onto the Garden floor. A reporter showed her an article that had appeared in the *New York Daily News*. One of the Queens College players had said that Nancy was overrated. She said Nancy wasn't as good as people were saying. Nancy felt hurt and upset.

"Why would someone who doesn't even know me say something bad about me?" Nancy thought. She shook her head and ran out onto the court with her teammates. She would just have to show her how good she was!

Nancy played about the best game of her life. It was like everyone else was playing in slow motion. She out jumped the others to get the rebounds. She made perfect passes to her teammates. And when she took the shot, it was almost as though she couldn't miss. Nancy scored 33 points. She made 14 out of 16 shots. Wow! Lady Magic. The girl was on fire.

Old Dominion was running Queens College right off the court. The player who had called Nancy over-rated was sitting at the end of the Queens' bench. She had a towel over her head, and she was staring down at her shoes.

"Do me a favor," her teammate said as she nudged her with an elbow. "If we ever play Lieberman's team again, keep your big mouth shut!"

Coach Stanley signaled for Nancy to come out of the game. "Way to go, Nancy." The coach gave her star point guard a quick hug. "Great game, Nancy." Nancy took a seat. She was tired and excited. The action on the court suddenly seemed far, far away. A deep quiet pushed out the noises and cheers of Madison Square Garden. Nancy thought she could almost hear the tinkling of piano music. She smiled. "Happy Birthday, Grandpa Lou."

● ● ●

It was almost midnight. Nancy and her roommate Rhonda Rompola were sitting around eating pizza and talking about their chances of winning the championship.

"Just get me the ball, Nancy," kidded her friend Rhonda. "Get me the ball and stand back and watch." Nancy laughed.

"Hey, how about another pizza?"

"Sure, double pepperoni, OK?"

"Let's make it a triple pepperoni!"

An hour later, Nancy and Rhonda were banging on the door of campus security.

"We need the keys to the field house," said Nancy.

"I gotta show this girl how to shoot a basketball,"

chimed in Rhonda.

"Ladies,- it's one o'clock in the morning," pleaded the security man.

"Never too late for basketball," said Nancy.

They played H-O-R-S-E. They played 21. They played full-court one on one. Both players were exhausted. Neither one would quit.

"Uh oh, you look a little green," Nancy said to Rhonda.

"You don't look so good yourself, kid," Rhonda answered.

Both women made a run to the bathroom holding their stomachs.

"You and your big ideas," gasped Nancy.

"Triple pepperoni," cried Rhonda.

"Ohhhhh!"

● ● ●

"It's just another game," Nancy kept telling herself. "It's just another game." But it wasn't just another game. This one was for the National Championship.

Old Dominion had defeated Billie Moore's UCLA team with a score of 87 to 82 in the semifinals. Now, they were here in Greensboro, North Carolina, to play Louisiana Tech for the championship of women's college basketball. For the first time, the women's championship game was going to be on television, live across the country.

Nancy was pacing back and forth in the locker room. She sat down. She stood up. She paced back and forth some more. Her teammates looked first at Nancy, and then at each other. What was going on here, anyway? Everyone depended on Nancy to be calm and steady. A serious case of nerves was spreading around the locker room like a bad cold, and everyone was catching it.

Nancy sat on the stool in front of her locker. She went through her regular pregame routine. First, she put on her left sock, then her right sock. She stepped into her shorts — left leg and then right leg. Then she put on her jersey. She always wore two wristbands — first the left one went on, and then the right one. Then, she put on her basketball shoes — the left and then the right.

Finally, she would carefully tape to her left leg the medal she had won her senior year in high school from the Public School Athletic League. She pulled her tube sock up over the medal.

"Let's go get 'em. It's just another game."

Only this time, the usual before-game jitters were hard to shake off. All the pressure was really getting to Nancy. It was getting to all of them. They started out slow and stiff. Nancy's pass bounced awkwardly off the shin of a surprised teammate. Rhonda's shot from behind the foul line hit the rim and was grabbed by Louisiana Tech. Inge was faked out by a head fake as Louisiana Tech's center went right by her for an easy basket.

Old Dominion was losing by 12 points at the half. "Ladies, let's relax out there," Coach Stanley encouraged her players. "Let's have some fun. Let's play our game."

Nancy bent over the sink to splash some cold water on her face. She looked up and saw herself in the locker room mirror. What she saw surprised her. Fear had been replaced by a fierce determination. Nancy was angry at herself. "You idiot," she told herself. "You're gonna blow it!"

And that's when it finally sunk in. This was really just another game — like thousands she had played on playgrounds all over New York, in gyms all across the country, and in huge arenas all over the world. Everyone else ran out of the locker room to play the second half, in front of a huge noisy crowd and the bright television lights. Nancy was going out there to play the game she loved to play — the game she had grown up playing in Far Rockaway years ago. It was just another game. Now she was ready.

Just before the half, Nancy had noticed that the other team's point guard had a bad habit when she played. As she turned her body, she'd leave the ball behind her. Nancy knew that a couple of quick steals and some fast-break baskets could turn the game around.

When the second half began, the Lady Monarchs started to play their game. Nancy led the charge up

and down the court. She wasn't going to stand around waiting for something good to happen. Nancy would make something good happen.

The Louisiana Tech point guard went into her spin move. Nancy came out of nowhere to flick the ball away. Rhonda grabbed the loose ball and raced down the court for a quick score. Basket by basket, Old Dominion chipped away at the lead. Again, the Tech guard made her move. Again, Nancy stole the ball. She bounce-passed it to Inge for the score.

The final buzzer sounded. The Lady Monarchs had won 75 to 65. They were the National Champions. Everyone was cheering and shouting. People were running all over the court. Cameras were flashing all over the Greensboro Coliseum. Nancy hugged Rhonda. She hugged her coach. She was so happy, tears were streaming down her cheeks.

There was Mom. Nancy ran over to her mother screaming, "Mom, Mom, can you believe it?" We're number one!" Nancy and her mom hugged and cried.

"Oh, Nancy," said Mrs. Lieberman. "I've always known that you were number one." A photographer stepped up to take the picture.

"Now, I guess the rest of the world knows it, too."

7

What Makes A Champion?

"I was just trouble as a kid. Just ask my mom and my teachers and my coaches. I loved to prove people wrong. All I would hear was, "You can't do that! You can't play sports like boys! You can't be on this team! You can't go into Harlem to play street ball!

"It gave me a lot of satisfaction to prove them wrong. If you want me to accomplish something, just tell me I can't.

"You girls are so really lucky to have wonderful female heroes to follow. I had heroes as a kid — but they were mostly guys named Willis, Walt and Julius.

"My little boy — T.J. — well, he just loves Cynthia Cooper." A loud roar went up from all the girls in the gym. They were cheering at the sound of the name of the Houston Comets' basketball all-star.

• • •

Nancy never got tired of that sound. For 16 years she had been running this camp just for girls to teach them all about basketball and life. She loved the way

they got so excited about basketball. It would have been a dream to come to a place like this as a kid. She was helping these new kids play out a dream. Watching them never failed to make her smile.

● ● ●

"What makes a champion?" Nancy shouted to the girls gathered at her feet.

"Winning!" said one little fourth grader.

"Being the best in the world!" a little pony-tailed girl answered.

"Nah," said Nancy. "A champion loves the game. A champion knows how to lose and bounce back to try again. A champion never stops trying to get better and help the team to get better. But most of all, a champion, a real champion, is the very best person off the court, too."

"Since you girls came here to the Nancy Lieberman-Cline Basketball Camp, you probably want me to teach you some basketball."

"Yea!" they all shouted in unison.

"OK, let's do one of my favorite drills. You're going to learn more about basketball than you ever imagined."

Nancy signaled to her assistant coaches to get the gym floor set up for the "chair drill." Chairs were being set up about 8 feet in front of the several baskets around the gym. The girls were guided to line up in single file groups behind the chairs. As the first girls took their seats with a basketball, Nancy gave the instructions.

"The purpose of the chair exercise is to teach you how to shoot the ball instead of just throwing it. Sitting in a chair will force you to keep your head up and focused on the basket. When I give the signal, I want each of you in the chairs to take 10 shots. Then give the ball to the next girl in line. OK — go!"

After each girl in line had a chance to sit in the chair and shoot, the coaches moved the chairs to the side of the baskets.

"Now, this time, I want you to concentrate on a spot above the rim. Make sure that you are extending your elbow. OK, let's go!'"

● ● ●

It was just so wonderful to watch these kids in action. Leading her summer camps was always a highlight of Nancy's year. She had dedicated her adult life to providing opportunities for girls in sports. Now, she was even the president of the Women's Sports Foundation. But this was all the time she could spend this summer. Tomorrow she was heading back to Detroit, Michigan to coach her team — the WNBA Detroit Shock. She would have to leave the coaching of these young girls to her great staff. Maybe, one day she would see a few of these young girls as stars in the WNBA.

● ● ●

Since she was 10 years old, nothing felt as good as playing basketball for Nancy. Next to playing basketball, Nancy loved coaching best. It takes a lot of patience and understanding to teach others the game that she knows so well.

Here at the Palace of Auburn Hills, Michigan, Nancy sure has a lot to do. Not only does she spend hours teaching her athletes how to become better basketball players, but she meets with her assistant coaches, watches films of games, and plans the team practices. She is responsible for a lot of people and a lot of action.

Here they were, gathered in the small gym across the parking lot from The Palace. Nancy was looking around at some of the best young female players in the country — Jennifer Azzi, Sandy Brondello, Wendy Palmer, and Dominique Canty. Nancy wondered how many of the younger players knew about her history as a player. Did they know that she had been the youngest basketball player ever to win a medal in the Olympics or that she had been the oldest player drafted into the WNBA when she played for the Phoenix Mercury in 1997?

She was about to teach them how she got so good. For practice today, Nancy and one of her coaches had put together a team of former male high school and college players. They call themselves the Tom Cross All-Stars. They would be practicing with the Shock to give the players a tougher scramble on the court. The job of the guys would be to never let the Shock players get an easy shot. It would teach the female players how to be a little more aggressive on the court, too. Nancy likes this kind of practice for her team because the guys are stronger and faster. She should know. She learned on the playgrounds with guys, and she even played in a men's professional league for two years.

Later that night Nancy was back in her office. From the girl with the tornado-struck room, Nancy has grown into a very, very, neat adult. Everything is in its place. All her pictures, newspaper articles and notes are in order. Even the large jar of red licorice has its own place on her desk. It's been a good day. She got everything done in preparation for tomorrow's trip to New York City and a game against the Liberty at Madison Square Garden. Now she can go home to Tim and T.J. and just be a regular mom for a few hours. Tomorrow morning, she will once again be Nancy Lieberman-Cline, one of the most accomplished individuals in the history of women's basketball.

• • •

The little birthday girl held hands with her dad. They stood in the Hall of Heroes on the third floor of the Basketball Hall of Fame in Springfield, Massachusetts. She was able to read the bronze plaque honoring Nancy Lieberman-Cline all by herself — with just a little help from her dad.

Elected to the Hall of Fame in 1996 with a prolific scoring ability and a fearless style on the court, Nancy Lieberman-Cline was a stand-out in women's amateur and professional basketball. At the age of 17, the native of Brooklyn, NY, emerged as a leader of an American team that took the gold medal in the Pan Am Games in 1975. In 1976, she became the youngest basketball player in Olympic history to win a medal — a silver medal for the U.S. team. A three-time All-American at Old Dominion University, Lieberman-Cline had a brilliant career in leading the Lady Monarchs to back-to-back AIAW National Championships, in 1979 and 1980 with a 72-2 record. Two times she was named the Wade Trophy winner — symbolic of the Women's National Player of the Year; the only two-time winner in history. Lieberman- Cline made history in 1986 and 1987 by becoming the first female to play in a men's professional league, signing with the Springfield Fame of the U.S. Basketball League. On September 21,1993, she became the first female ever inducted into the New York City Basketball Hall of Fame.

On the second floor of the Basketball Hall of Fame the little girl discovered a wonderful exhibit. It was called "Heart & Soul — A Celebration of Women's Professional Basketball." There were some terrific mementos honoring the greats of women's basketball. The 10-year old pointed excitedly to Nancy Lieberman's game jersey from the WABA Dallas Diamonds. Of course, it was Nancy's old #10, and it was white with a blue trim. There were also Nancy's jersey and old basketball shoes from the Springfield Fame, the men's team she played on.

A television monitor played an old video of Nancy Lieberman on the court. The young girl laughed. Everything looked so old-fashioned. The uniform shorts were really short, and Nancy wore knee-high white socks. But she could see how fast Nancy played. She watched as Nancy grabbed a rebound, turned, and made a pass, all in one motion. The Hall-of-Famer looked very strong and very determined. It was easy to see what made Nancy such a winner.

Down the hall from the Heart & Soul exhibit was a row of baskets. Visitors were allowed to test their basketball skills. The little girl eyed the basket and took careful aim. She bounced the ball a couple of times, the way she had seen Jennifer Azzi do it last night at Madison Square Garden. Oops! Air ball. The shot fell way short. She took a deep breath and tried again. The ball hit the back of the rim and shot straight up into the air and over the backboard.

Last shot. The score was tied with no time left on the clock. The youthful ball player imagined that she was Nancy Lieberman playing for the U.S. Olympic team. She bounced the ball and took careful aim. The ball cleared the front rim and fell through the net. Swish! The birthday girl and her dad both had big smiles. They gave each other a high-five, smacking their hands in the air.

"Dad, when I grow up, I want to be just like Nancy." The father gave his daughter a big birthday hug.

Nancy Lieberman-Cline's Career Highlights

♦ Youngest basketball player (age 18) in Olympic history to win a medal (1976 silver medal)
♦ Named to the Olympic basketball team again in 1980
♦ Member of the U.S. National Team (1976-1980)
♦ Member of the Pan-American teams (1975 gold medal, 1979 silver medal)
♦ Member of the World Championship teams (1975, 1979 gold medal)
♦ All-American at Old Dominion University (1978-1980)
♦ Outstanding Female Athlete of the Year at ODU (1977-1980)
♦ The only two-time winner of the Wade Trophy for most-outstanding college player
♦ Recipient of the Broderick Cup for the nation's top female basketball player (1979)
♦ First woman to play in a men's professional league — the USBL's Springfield Fame (1986)
♦ Played professionally in the WABA for the Dallas Diamonds (1981, 1984)

- ♦ Inducted to the Naismith Memorial Basketball Hall of Fame (1996)
- ♦ Played professionally in the WNBA for the Phoenix Mercury (1997)
- ♦ Coach and general manager of the WNBA Detroit Shock (1998-present)
- ♦ President of the Women's Sports Foundation
- ♦ Inducted to the Women's Basketball Hall of Fame (1999)

Above all, Nancy says the biggest highlights of her life are her husband, Tim Cline, and their son, T.J.

Sports Talk

To Parents, Teachers, and Coaches:

In this section you will find a discussion of some of the issues presented by Nancy's story as a young female athlete. We also share with you some information about the influence of sports participation on girls, and we have suggested some discussion questions for you. We encourage you to talk about these topics with the young reader. Starting a dialogue and exchanging ideas can enhance this story for the soon-to-be athlete and make the sports experience more enjoyable for the young, accomplished athlete.

It's OK for Girls to Be Competitive

Nancy had a powerful competitive drive that pushed her to succeed in spite of the obstacles in her way. Sports can teach healthy competitive and cooperative attitudes. The emphasis should be on the inner rewards of competition, such as learning how to make decisions, leadership training, meeting challenges and working with others. Competitive sports can teach girls to be strategic, to plan ahead, to relax under stress, to concentrate and stay focused. Training for and competing in sports requires a commitment. From this commitment of time and effort, a young girl learns how to set goals, take responsibility and prepare for the challenges of life. She has the opportunity to learn how to accept failure and be a gracious winner while enjoying the thrill of success.

Boys have traditionally been rewarded and praised for their competitive endeavors. Shouldn't girls also be allowed to experience the achievements and the teamwork and the glory? There are some hazards to placing a child in an overly competitive environment. It should be age-appropriate. It should be either stress-free, or the young person should be taught anxiety-reducing skills. There should be lots of positive feedback. Help the young athlete to find something good about each difficult practice and competition. Remember to keep it fun — the most important element of youth sports.

Q: Nancy loved to play sports, and she really loved to win. How does it feel to win? How does it feel to lose? Do you think that losing would make Nancy stop playing basketball?

Body Image

Nancy felt awkward about how strong and muscular she was compared to the other girls at school. She was teased about looking like a boy. For a while it really upset her when the other kids teased her.

94

Youngsters become aware of being fat or thin at a very early age. Both boys and girls can have distorted self-images about what they should look like. A lot of that has to do with the images they see in magazines and on television. Most girls are uncomfortable with what they look like. Most think, incorrectly, that they are overweight.

Nancy gained a lot of confidence from being a great athlete. Along with this, she began to feel more secure about how healthy and powerful her body was. She realized that this is what athletes can look like.

Girls are generally more negative about their bodies than boys. Girls can learn through sport to view their bodies in a positive way. Basketball really helped Nancy to have a strong and healthy body image.

Q: Think of different sports — gymnastics, shot-put, pole-vault, weight-lifting, figure-skating. What would your body have to look like to do well in these sports? What part of your body do you like the best?

Lack of Family Support

It was tough for Nancy when other moms and dads would come to the basketball games to watch their kids playing. It took a long time for Nancy's family to appreciate her talent and achievements. In fact, they kept trying to talk her out of playing basketball. Nothing would stop her, though. The coaches and the sports teams became her family, too.

Nancy is a real exception. In most cases, a young girl will not stay motivated to pursue sports without her family's support. It is an important part of the sports experience for young athletes. The love and encouragement of family members can help the young girl enjoy the victories and accept the defeats. The family can be a part of a child's love affair with sports. They can take great pride in her accomplishments. They can provide a shoulder and a hug for the setbacks. At the same time, the family needs to be careful to avoid putting extra stress on the young athlete, especially during that post-game analysis. After all, it's supposed to be fun.

Q: Nancy was able to follow her dream and become a great athlete. Can you imagine yourself as a superstar athlete? What would that be like?

Competing Against the Boys

One of the issues for young Nancy was being the only girl on most of her early teams. The boys were happy to have Nancy on their team — because of her talent, but the adults in Nancy's life had a difficult time accepting her enthusiasm for sports. Times have changed, and today we often find girls and boys are competing together on a sports team.

For some girls, it may be a better decision to play in an all-girls league. In many cases, girls learn fundamental sports skills later than boys. They may feel sensitive about their lack of skills. For some girls, the friendships and social interaction are the best part of sports. They may feel less intimidated about taking risks on an all-girls team.

Other girls may find playing with and against the boys is a real advantage. A co-ed situation allows boys and girls to play at a higher level of competition. In teen years, boys are generally taller, heavier and stronger than girls. But in many sports this is not a major problem. In basketball, Nancy needed speed, agility and coordination to be successful. To have fair co-ed teams, young athletes should be grouped according to skill level and size rather than sex.

Q: What sports are boys and girls both good at? What sports do you think women are better at? What sports do you think men are better at?

Difficulties with the Coach

Nancy had some wonderful experiences with supportive coaches until her first college coach. She just didn't get along with her. It made Nancy feel miserable, and she almost quit playing basketball. Luckily, there were other people who helped Nancy stay involved with basketball.

Sometimes personalities clash. After all, both athletes and coaches are human. It is so important to talk over problems and issues before they become a big deal. Learn the best way to communicate with the coach about something that is causing trouble. Expressing feelings may even help to bring the coach and athlete closer together.

Once in a while, an athlete may find herself in a situation with a coach whom she just does not click with. The tension between the two just seems to grow and grow. If, after trying to communicate and making an effort to get along, it is still not working, the athlete may have to look around for another situation. Better to turn toward another coach than to turn off from the sport.

If there is no other team or coach around, learning how to get through the situation can become a valuable life lesson. Get as much support as possible from family and friends for the young athlete and help her to stick it out, rather than give up the sport she adores. Keep reminding her of all the things she loves about playing her sport.

Q: What are some things a coach might do that would upset you? How would you be different if you were the coach?

The Benefits of Sports Participation for Girls:

More than ever before, American girls are actively involved in sports. Recent research has demonstrated the importance and value of exercise and sports for girls. These lessons learned in childhood help to shape the developing adult. Sports influence girls' physical health, psychological well-being, overall social development and academic achievement.

Girls have a difficult time these days — many have overwhelming concerns about their competence, self-worth and body image. Regular participation in exercise and sports programs provides tangible experiences of achievement that teach girls problem-solving skills and promote self-confidence. Through the influence of healthy role models and interaction with teammates, young athletes learn how to deal with failure and how to create expectations of success.

Involvement in sports and the development of an identity as an athlete help a young girl get through the everyday stresses by increasing self-esteem, lowering tension and teaching her how to better handle challenges. Being physically active helps to create a healthy body image. Being an athlete also encourages girls to avoid risky actions and learn responsible social behaviors. It can also be an antidote to such social problems as teen pregnancy, substance abuse and violent behaviors.

Sports are an educational asset in girls' lives. Research findings show that high school female athletes report higher grades and lower drop-out rates and are more likely to go on to college than their non-athlete counterparts. Team sports and the competitive arena are a natural place to learn the lessons of positive conflict resolution. The universal character of sport helps to break down barriers, challenge stereotypes and act as a tool for tolerance.

General discussion questions:

What do you think makes playing sports fun?

Who are your heroes in sports?

What makes her/him special?

What do you need to be good at sports?

How do you get ready to play your sport?

What do you worry about when you play sports?

What is the most important part of playing your sport?

How important is winning? Would you do anything to win?

What happens when you lose?

Women's Basketball

Basketball is one of the most popular sports for girls in the United States. There are more opportunities for female basketball players now than ever before. Collegiate basketball has become a real favorite with the fans. There are more scholarships for women. Television coverage has expanded. There is a professional league, the WNBA. It is easier to follow your favorite teams and players. There are now instructional and club opportunities through the YWCA and the Girls Scouts of America.

PROGRAMS

USA Basketball is the national governing body for men's and women's basketball in the United States. It is responsible for the selection, training and fielding of USA teams that compete in various national and international competitions:

- ◆ The Olympic Games (The USA Women have captured the gold three times)
- ◆ International Basketball Federation (FIBA) World Championships
- ◆ Pan American Games

- World University Games
- Junior National Team — for men and women 19 years old and younger
- USA Basketball Select Teams — to develop younger talent

A BRIEF HISTORY OF WOMEN'S BASKETBALL

1893: The first official women's basketball game is played at Smith College

1926: The first AAU National Women's Basketball Championship is played

1955: The USA women's basketball team competes in the Pan-American Games

1969: The first National Intercollegiate Women's Basketball Tournament is played at West Chester University

1971: A five-player, full court game, with a 30-second clock is introduced

1975: The first Kodak All-American team is named

1976: The first Olympic competition in women's basketball is held in Montreal

1979: The first nationally televised game is aired. Old Dominion beats Louisiana Tech

1980: Cheryl Miller is the first female to dunk in a high school game

1982: The first NCAA National Championships for women are held

1984: The USA Women's Basketball Team wins the Olympic gold medal in Los Angeles

1988: The USA Women's Basketball Team wins the Olympic gold medal in Seoul

1985: Lynette Woodard becomes the first woman to play with the Harlem Globetrotters

1986: Nancy Lieberman becomes the first woman to play in a men's professional league — the Springfield Fame in the USBL

1992: Kodak sponsors the first All-American game for high school girls

1993: The Women's Basketball Hall of Fame is established in Jackson, Tennessee

1996: The USA Women's Basketball Team wins the Olympic gold medal in Atlanta

Resources

Resources for girls and women's sports and fitness information:

The Women's Sports Foundation:
www.womensportsfoundation.org

Just Sports for Women:
www.SportsforWomen.com

The Melponeme Institute:
www.melponeme.org

GirlPower! Sports & Fitness
www.health.org/gpower

Resources For Basketball Information:

United States Olympic Committee:
www.usoc.org/sports
The USOC now has an area on their website called "Where do I Play?" that will list clubs for sports in your area.

United States Basketball Association:
www.usabasketball.com

If you are interested in finding a local program, this is another resource:

Amateur Athletic Union (AAU):
www.aaugirlsbasketball.org
The AAU has been a leader in providing competitive opportunities from the local to the national level. The programs range from ages 10 and under to post college.

Women's Basketball Coaches Association:
www.wbca.org

Women's National Basketball Association
(WNBA): www.wnba.com

The Women's Basketball Hall of Fame:
www.wbhof.com

Naismith Memorial Basketball Hall of Fame:
www.hoophall.com

Glossary

Accomplished: successful; finished something successfully

Aggressive: very bold, pushy and energetic

All-American: honorary title given to the very best athletes in college

Amateur: a person who does something for enjoyment, not money

Aspiring: hoping to become something

Asthma: an illness, usually due to an allergy, in which there are attacks of wheezing, coughing and hard breathing

Bayonet: a large knife attached to the front of a rifle

Bleachers: a section of seats that are benches in rows, one above the other

Boroughs: the five main divisions of New York City

Campus security: a college police officer

Collegiate: having to do with college or university

Competitive: having to do with enjoying being in a contest with others; wanting to win

Concession stand: game or food booth at an amusement park, sporting event or fair

Consciousness: the condition of being awake, and aware of your surroundings

Cross-over dribble: a move in basketball that involves bouncing the ball and switching from one hand to the other

Deafening: overwhelming with too much noise

Defense: the side in a game of basketball that defends the basket against the other team scoring a point

Double-team: two defensive players guard a single offensive player

Drafted: a college player selected by a professional team

Dribble: to move the ball in basketball by using short bounces

Fast-break: trying to get down court to the basket to score, before the other team gets there to defend

Focused: paying strict attention to; concentrated on

Freshman: a first year student in high school or college

Encouragement: the act of making someone feel more confident

Inside-outside combination: a basketball play between the center and the guard

Insurance: a contract from a company to pay a certain amount of money in case someone is hurt

Jubilantly: proudly and joyfully

Junior: a third-year student in high school or college

Layup: a shot in basketball, close up to the basket, bounced off the backboard

Man-to-man defense: each player is assigned a specific opponent to defend

Mementos: items that are tokens of something special to remember

Oarlocks: holders on the sides of the row boat that keep the oars in place

Offense: the side with the ball in a basketball game, trying to score

Olympics: international sports competition held every four years

One-three-one zone: a type of zone defense

Peripheral: on the edge, the outer, the surrounding

Physically: having to do with the body

Pick-up games: neighborhood sports games without officials or coaches

Pirouettes: spinning dance movement with the body

Plaque: a flat piece of metal with lettering on it used to honor someone

Point guard: a position on the basketball team responsible for setting up the play

Professional: earning a living from playing a sport

Prolific: producing a lot

Rallied: came from behind

Rebound: when a player gets possession of a missed shot

Retrieve: to find and get something back

Sandlot: an unorganized, neighborhood game of baseball

Scanned: looked over quickly

Scrimmage: game play in practice

Souvenir: an object that is kept as a reminder of something

Spunky: brave

Squad: team

Standings: a listing of the won-loss record of the teams

Street ball: neighborhood basketball games in playgrounds and schoolyards

Strategy: a game plan

Swap: to trade

Tomboy: a negative name for girls who really like playing sports

Tornado: a storm of whirling wind that usually destroys everything in its path

Tournament: a series of contests or competitions

Transistor radio: a small cordless radio that runs on batteries

Two-on-one break: type of fast break with two players trying to score and only one opponent there to defend

Zone defense: each player is assigned a certain portion of the court to defend

About the Authors

Dr. Doreen Greenberg is a certified consultant in sport psychology and has worked with school, college, professional and Olympic athletes from a variety of sports. These experiences have ranged from consulting with national and world champions to helping young children with their initial fears about training and competition. Dr. Greenberg was a primary author of *Physical Activity and Sport in the Lives of Girls* (1997), a report for the President's Council on Physical Fitness and Sports; an associate editor of *The Encyclopedia of Women and Sport in America* (Oryx Press, 1998), and editor of *Sport in the Lives of Urban Girls* (Women's Sports Foundation, 1998).

Michael A. Greenberg is a former English teacher and retired business executive. While going to college in the Boston area in the late 1960's, he attended every Sixers-Celtics game at the old Boston Garden. Unfortunately, he was supposed to be attending classes at the time.

Michael and Doreen have two grown daughters and live at the New Jersey shore with their three dogs.

Did You Enjoy This Book?

Be sure to look for other titles in the *Anything You Can Do ...* series:

A Drive to Win: The Story of Nancy Lieberman-Cline
(isbn: 1-930546-40-8)

Sword of a Champion: The Story of Sharon Monplaisir
(isbn: 1-930546-39-4)

And coming in 2001:

Fast Lane to Victory: The Story of Jenny Thompson
(isbn: 1-930546-38-6)

Gold in Her Glove: The Story of Julie Smith
(isbn: 1-930546-37-8)

For information about these and other quality Wish Publishing titles, check out our website:
www.wishpublishing.com